ABSALOM JONES

AMERICA'S FIRST BLACK PRIEST

ABSALOM JONES
AMERICA'S FIRST BLACK PRIEST

MARK FRANCISCO BOZZUTI-JONES

Illustrated by

CHRISTOPHER MICHAEL TAYLOR

Morehouse Publishing
NEW YORK

Church Publishing Incorporated
19 East 34th Street
New York, NY 10016

Cover design by Christopher Michael Taylor
Typeset by Progressive Publishing Services

Library of Congress Cataloging-in-Publication Data
A record of this book is available from the Library of Congress.

ISBN-13: 978-1-64065-472-3 (paperback)
ISBN-13: 978-1-64065-473-0 (ebook)

Dedicated to Kathy and Mark Anthony Bozzuti-Jones

and

Black Christians throughout the world.

Mark Francisco Bozzuti-Jones

I dedicate this work to my mother,

Audrey Chaney Taylor.

Christopher Michael Taylor

Introduction: Absalom Jones and the Faith Heritage of Black Christians

Absalom Jones is a son of Africa, a descendant of a faithful people. Since the beginning, Africans have known God.

God was in Africa from the moment of creation and continues to be in Africa today.

Africans, from the whole of Africa, with diverse tribes and cultures, have always practiced their faith in God as Creator and Sustainer of all that is, seen and unseen.

Africans practiced their faith in God by honoring nature: giving special respect to the mysteries of life manifested in plants, the creatures of the seas and air, the animals in the forest and wilderness, the power in nature and the weather, and in all the mysteries of life.

They practiced their faith in God by loving each other, respecting the things they did not understand, living their lives to the best of their ability, honoring the ancestors, learning from other peoples, and striving to be good stewards of the earth.

In honoring God since the beginning, they tried their best to live *Ubuntu*, a word that can be translated as "I am because we are," and to live the golden rule of treating others the way they want to be treated. They tried to honor God and each other and ensure that life had meaning for each person.

They also believed in learning from other cultures and different religions. Like all human beings, they had moments when they turned away, disobeyed God, and failed to practice the way of love.

It is important to remember that, since the beginning of time, there have always been Africans who remained faithful to God and who have been called as prophets, saints, martyrs, and evangelists. There have always been righteous, saintly, and faithful Africans. And with the passage of time, Africans encountered many other religious faith traditions.

African countries are present in the Hebrew scriptures: Ethiopia, Egypt, and Libya. African Jews are as old as Judaism itself. In Acts 8:26–40, we read the story of an Ethiopian eunuch who converts to Christianity. He is the first individual convert to Christianity, and he is African.

What this tells us is that Judaism and Christianity existed in Africa long before they existed in many European countries.

God, faith, and Christianity existed in Africa long before the arrival of Europeans.

When the European slave traders and colonizers arrived in Africa, many Africans were practicing Jews, Christians, and Muslims, as well as practitioners of all manner of indigenous religious practices. Africans treasured and practiced their faith with devotion, reverence, and commitment.

Among the captured slaves brought to the Americas (the United States of America, Jamaica, Brazil, Colombia, and Cuba, to name a few) were practicing Christians who knew the story of the enslavement of the Hebrew people, and they knew how Christians had been persecuted and crucified by Rome.

Their faith in God and their knowledge of how faithful people had been persecuted for hundreds and thousands of years prepared them for their journey from Africa, where they were shackled in the bottomless pits of slave ships, arrived in strange lands, and lived as persecuted and enslaved people.

Even in the most dehumanizing and soul-stealing situations, the Africans held fast to their faith. They sang their faith and practiced their faith. The Christian slaves encouraged each other to remain faithful to God and they passed on their faith: they sang Spirituals, read the Bible, shared the Scriptures they had memorized, and remembered that they were beloved children of God.

This is the lineage of Absalom Jones. It is to people such as these that Absalom Jones was born.

Slaves were often forced to follow the religion of their owners. So, a Roman Catholic, Baptist, Methodist, Lutheran, or Anglican owner would have insisted that the slaves observed the same religious practices.

The slave master of Absalom Jones was an Anglican. Absalom Jones learned the Anglican faith and practiced the Anglican faith. He accepted the Anglican faith as the path in which God wanted to lead him. At its root was the legacy of faith from his parents, grandparents, and a family tree of ancestors, stretching all the way back to Africa.

ABSALOM JONES

AMERICA'S FIRST BLACK PRIEST

1 Born into Slavery

Absalom Jones was born on February 8, 1746, about midway between the time when the first slave ship arrived in North America and when slavery finally became illegal in the United States.

Between 1619 and 1865, more than five million people from Africa were kidnapped, sold, enslaved, and shipped to America, making the era one of the ugliest and most brutal periods in history.

Enslaved people were sold as property. Those who bought them thought of them as objects, not people. They tried to tell the enslaved ones that they were subhuman, and that God wanted them to be that way.

Many slave traders used the Bible to justify their evil actions, even though that is not what the Bible teaches. Look at the Golden Rule in Matthew 7:12, where Jesus commands us to love one another and to do to others as we would like them to do to us.

Enslaved people worked in the sugar, cotton, and tobacco fields to enrich their captors. The labor was harsh and brutal. They also built schools, churches, homes, government buildings, and provided the main workforce in America, even though they didn't get to take advantage of most of what they had built.

They were forced to work long hours in the hot sun. If anyone tried to escape, they were brutally beaten, often publicly punished, and sometimes killed. However, many enslaved people managed to escape, and many others risked their lives to help them do it.

Of course, the enslaved brought their varying tribal cultures and religious traditions with them from Africa. They had faith in God and carried deep within them the desire for freedom and a good life. Absalom Jones was born into slavery.

■

2 A Special Child

Absalom Jones was born in Sussex County, Delaware. Because his mother was enslaved, he, too, was considered a slave from the moment he was born. It was raining the day his mother went into labor, and it kept raining until the next day, making the fields too wet for anyone to work.

An elderly couple who helped deliver Absalom presented him to his mother and said, "This child will be special. Among your seven children, he will be a light and a true servant of God. He will bring God's peace, justice, and freedom to many. Absalom will be a child of goodness, truth, and beauty. He will show God's love to all who meet him."

His mother remembered all these things and pondered them in her heart.

As Absalom's mother held her son in her arms, she prayed that God would protect him and make him a servant and a man of peace. She cried because she knew the many dangers of slavery. But as a woman of faith, she believed in her heart that God would protect her child. She also offered her son to God, as she had done for all her children.

Every day his mother asked God to protect Absalom and make him a child of goodness, truth, and beauty — to make him a person of peace. As she fed him and nurtured him, she told him Bible stories about the ways God protected and freed the people of Israel. She also told him stories of the enslaved people who committed their lives to attaining freedom for others.

Absalom grew in wisdom and stature, in favor with God and all the people who met him. People spoke about his determination, kindness, and bravery, even as a child. He worked hard to be helpful to his parents and his friends. More than anything else, he loved to listen to the Bible stories and sing songs in worship.

■

3 Singing in the Fields

Absalom went to work in the fields with his mother every day. In the middle of the harsh conditions of their labor, Absalom was a peaceful presence that affected everyone around him, even as a boy. Children jostled to work alongside him. He taught them the songs and stories he had learned.

While the people worked, they sang as well to pass the time and lift their spirits—songs we have come to know as Spirituals because of their deep meaning. One day, Absalom Jones witnessed the slave masters whipping a man who had tried to escape. As they beat him, the man sang, "When Israel was in Egypt's land, let my people go. Oppressed so hard they could not stand. Let my people go." The other enslaved people who had gathered at a distance joined in: "Go down, Moses. Way down in Egypt's land. Tell ol' Pharaoh. Let my people go."

The people sang songs that described a mighty God, their homeland in Africa, and their hopes for deliverance. When the Hebrew people were enslaved in Egypt, they never lost their faith in the God of their fathers and mothers. They, too, sang praises to God and sang their hopes for deliverance.

It was in those fields where Absalom learned the haunting sounds of Spirituals like "Wade in the Water," "Swing Low, Sweet Chariot," "Sometimes I Feel Like a Motherless Child," "Nobody Knows the Trouble I've Seen," "Every Time I Feel the Spirit," "Let Us Break Bread Together on Our Knees," and "Steal Away." Christians still sing these Spirituals today. There were many other songs of hope and faith, joy and sorrow, as well as stories about life in Africa.

"Steal Away," "Swing Low, Sweet Chariot," and

"Nobody Knows the Troubles I've Seen" were three of

his favorite spirituals. After supper each night, Absalom

Jones would sing for his family and preach to them.

His singing and preaching delighted his family and

gave them hope. His voice would often tremble when

he sang the phrase from *Steal Away*, "We ain't got

long to stay here."

Absalom never tired of reciting Bible verses and sharing

them with everyone.

Some of his favorite passages were:

> *And the Lord said, I have surely seen the oppression of my people which are in Egypt and have heard their cry by reason of their taskmasters; for I know their sorrows; and I am come down to deliver them out of the hand of the Egyptians, and to bring them up out of that land unto a good land.*
>
> *Beloved, let us love one another, because love is from God and everyone who loves is born of God. The one who does not love does not know God, for God is love. O, beloved, let us love one another.*
>
> *Jesus said, I have come that you may have life and have it more abundantly.*
>
> *And I say to you, do good to those that hate you. Love your enemies.*
>
> *Whatever you do to the least, you do to me.*
>
> *Love one another.*

Absalom Jones talked about these verses his whole life.

He also taught the Lord's Prayer and the 23rd Psalm, "The Lord is my Shepherd . . ."

One day he was walking home from his master's store and saw two elderly slaves fighting. They were from different tribes in Africa. Absalom stepped in the middle of the two men and separated them. He said, "Do not be the cause of your own destruction. Love one another and forgive each other. Remember, blessed are the peacemakers for they shall be called the children of God."

Three days later, he saw two teenage slaves crying because they were afraid of their masters. He told them, "Jesus said, do not fear those who can only kill the body. Do not fear them." He encouraged them to keep their faith strong when it was tested, be courageous, and trust in God.

A week after that, he visited a group of women whose husbands had been killed by the slave masters. He consoled them by singing, "Were you there when they crucified my Lord?" Their hearts were healed; they felt comforted in Absalom's consoling presence. He reminded them that Jesus knew their troubles and also knew how it felt to be abandoned.

The man who owned Absalom's family was a rich plantation owner in Delaware. He was also an Anglican who attended church faithfully. The Anglican Church, the primary religious group in England during the time of slavery, was one of the main religious groups of the slaveholders and American colonists.

The slave owner noticed Absalom's intelligence and peaceful demeanor and took Absalom from working in the fields to work in the house.

■

4 A Family Torn Apart

At a young age, Absalom Jones learned the importance of saving money and also giving an offering in the church, even though his family didn't have much money. When the slave master sent him to the market to do shopping, Absalom always accounted for the money and returned the change. Many times, the master told Absalom to keep the change because he had been so honest. Absalom saved the money and was able to buy a spelling book, a prayer book, and a Bible of his own. He treasured and read them all his life.

Because he worked in the house, Absalom had more opportunity to read the Bible as well as some other books that belonged to the slave owner. By his thirteenth birthday, Absalom had read the Bible three times and had practically memorized the hymnal and prayer book. He also learned to add, subtract, and keep track of money. In other words, he taught himself accounting.

All the white visitors to the house commented on how thoughtful, earnest, and intelligent he was. But even though the master appeared to favor him, Absalom was nothing but property to his owner. Shortly after Absalom's sixteenth birthday, his master sold him, his sister, his five brothers, and his mother to a neighboring plantation owner.

The new owner kept the gifted Absalom to work for him and resold the rest of the family. On the day they were separated from each other, they hugged and cried because they knew they would never see one another again.

His mother sang a song of eternal hope:

> *Sometimes I feel discouraged/ And think my work's in vain/ But then the Holy Spirit/ Revives my soul again. / If you can preach like Peter/ If you can pray like Paul/ Go home and tell your loved ones/ He died to save us all.*

Absalom hugged his family and blessed them. He wept and told them he loved them, reminding them that God would be in them and that they should go in peace through their troubles.

His mother said, "There's a balm in Gilead. Don't forget what is good, true, and beautiful. Don't forget that your name means 'father of peace.' The peace of the Lord be always with you."

Together they responded, "And with your spirit."

■

5   On to Philadelphia

Absalom was taken to Philadelphia. His new owner, also

an Anglican, was a member of St. Peter's Church. This

owner attended church regularly and was a member of

the vestry. Absalom went to church as often as he was

allowed. Absalom worked at his owner's store, selling

produce and goods made by enslaved people. He

attended a night school for slaves run by the Quakers,

who opposed slavery. They marveled at his compassion,

wisdom, and holiness.

When he was twenty, Absalom Jones married Mary

Thomas, who was also enslaved. The men who owned

them had to give permission for them to be married.

Absalom promised Mary that they would be free one day. He planned to buy her freedom before he paid for his own. If she were free, by law their children would be born free. Absalom dreamed of freedom for not only his family but for all Black people.

Absalom worked extra jobs and saved his money for many years. With help from his father-in-law and the Quakers, he purchased Mary's freedom. He kept saving money and bought his own freedom, as well as a piece of land and a house. Since he bought the house while he was still enslaved, they put it in Mary's name, because a slave was not allowed to own property.

Even though Absalom earned enough money, his master would not grant his freedom. But Absalom kept working and praying, and God heard his prayer.

When Absalom was thirty-eight years old, the slave owner granted his freedom. Even though he kept working in his former master's store—now as a paid employee—he quit using the slave owner's last name. He chose the name Jones, because it sounded to him like the name of a free American.

■

6 The Free African Society

In 1793, a three-month yellow fever epidemic killed many in the white community. Some physicians thought that Black people were immune from the epidemic, but that was just a way to make them take care of the white people during the outbreak.

Absalom Jones worked tirelessly and without pay to tend to the sick. Many white people credited him with saving their lives. His courageous efforts endeared him even more to the white population, and many celebrated his extraordinary goodness.

Once he became freed from slavery, Absalom Jones was no longer allowed to attend the slave owner's church, so he began to worship at St. George's Methodist Episcopal Church where he met another former slave, Richard Allen. They became great friends. They founded the Free African Society to teach their people how to save money and how to invest, so they could buy property.

The two friends collected money to feed the hungry, help the sick, care for prisoners, and help enslaved people buy their freedom. They encouraged each other and together they practiced following Jesus's way of love.

More and more enslaved people came to St. George's because of the preaching and ministry of Richard Allen and Absalom Jones.

Many white members of the church got angry that too many free Black people and slaves were attending the church. Some of the leaders in the church decided it was time to segregate the congregation and have the Black people sit in a different section.

One day without warning, white parishioners and vestrymen dragged Absalom, Richard, and some other Black worshipers out of their pews while they were praying and threw them out of the church. The remaining Black people got up and walked out singing, "We Shall Overcome Some Day."

Shocked and disappointed about how the white members
of the church had treated them, Absalom, Richard,
and the other Black people had to find a new place to
worship.

Even though Richard and Absalom were best friends,
they disagreed about what to do next.

Absalom did not want to leave the Anglican church, but
Richard said he could no longer worship in a tradition
that embarrassed them so badly, in the middle of a
worship service. Richard Allen left the Anglican Church
and founded the African Methodist Episcopal Church
in 1794. He and Absalom remained great friends. They
continued their work together for the freedom of slaves
and an end to the separation of enslaved families.

Absalom and those who felt that he was their spiritual leader agreed to find or build a church, where they could continue to worship in the Anglican tradition.

7   Starting a Church

The African Church was dedicated on July 17, 1794.
It was part of the Episcopal Church, the American
expression of Anglicanism after the Revolutionary War.

The white people insisted that the Black worshipers
could not attend church conventions or get involved
with church governance, even though they were in the
same denomination. They made the Black worshipers
promise that they would not try to integrate the
churches and would only worship in the churches
provided for them.

Absalom Jones was granted the authority to control the affairs of his church. The Episcopal Bishop granted him permission to preach and give pastoral care.

People loved to hear him preach. In his sermons, Absalom always found a way to include these words of Jesus:

> *Love one another. I have come that you might have abundant life. God has seen our oppression. Do not be afraid. Be good. Be not afraid. Blessed are the peacemakers.*

Absalom continued to serve his people with compassion, respect, and love, ministering to their needs. Many who met him loved him and felt transformed by his ministry. The impact of his healing ministry remains his legacy to this day.

◼

8 America's First Black Priest

Bishop William White ordained Absalom Jones as a deacon in 1795. As a deacon, Absalom Jones was tasked to teach, preach, and guide his congregation. Just as he had done his whole life long, Absalom encouraged the church members to pray and to remain hopeful. He encouraged them to believe in God with all their heart, mind, soul, and strength.

On September 21, 1802, Absalom was ordained a priest—to serve in the church he founded. He and his congregants proudly named their church, The African Episcopal Church of St. Thomas.

Episcopal Church rules required that deacons and priests

study Greek and Latin, but the requirement was waived

for Absalom Jones, so as not to delay his ordination.

He made it clear to those who questioned him that

he knew the Bible, the prayer book, the hymnal, and

several African languages well. He spoke with authority,

without shaming or blaming, and always with love.

These were the words from one of his early sermons:

> "Arise out of the dust and shake ourselves, and
> throw off that servile fear, that the habit of oppression
> and bondage trained us up in. And in meekness and
> fear, we would desire to walk in the liberty where
> with Christ has made us free."

Occasionally, Absalom was invited to preach at a white parish or in a white home, where he had the courage to preach, "Clean your hands of slaves." He reminded them that God could see the oppression caused by slavery and that God always acted on behalf of the oppressed and distressed.

Many in the white church objected to Absalom Jones preaching about freedom, but he was such a notable preacher that they left him alone. They could find no fault in him.

Absalom Jones made pastoral visits almost every
day. He had a kind word and gesture for everyone
he met along the way. People looked to his visits for
encouragement. He called them to look to God and to
keep on believing in the freedom, justice, and love
that were their birthright.

Notably, Absalom devoted two nights a week to teaching
enslaved people to read, which expanded his work of
doing good for others by preparing them for freedom.
He encouraged them to read the Bible and to be steadfast
in their belief that freedom would come. Whenever he
met young children, he encouraged them to read, too.

He had a special ministry for mothers who had been
separated from their children. He helped them to find
a peace deep within themselves, in spite of their loss.
Indeed, Absalom had lived up to this name, "father
of peace."

In the year before he died, Absalom Jones founded a literary organization, the Augustine Society. To his last breath, Absalom Jones believed strongly in the priority of developing the mind as a first step toward freedom.

Rain fell all day when Absalom Jones died on February 13, 1818. He was buried in the African Episcopal Church of St. Thomas churchyard.

In his lifetime, he served his people and the Church well, and he continues to offer inspiration today to those who work for peace, justice, and freedom, and walk in goodness, truth, and beauty.

In his memory, we pray:

Set us free, Loving God, from every bond of prejudice and fear; that honoring the steadfast courage of your servant Absalom Jones, we may show forth in our lives the reconciling love and true freedom of the children of God, which you have given us in your Son our Savior Jesus Christ; who lives and reigns with you and the Holy Spirit, one God, now and forever.

Amen.

Timeline of African Americans and the Episcopal Church

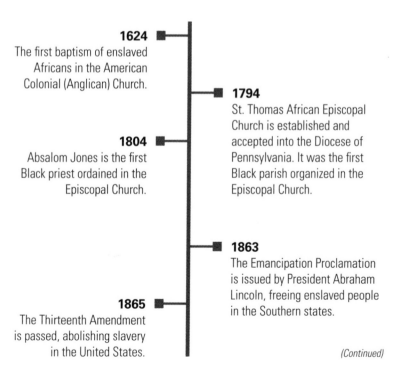

1624
The first baptism of enslaved Africans in the American Colonial (Anglican) Church.

1794
St. Thomas African Episcopal Church is established and accepted into the Diocese of Pennsylvania. It was the first Black parish organized in the Episcopal Church.

1804
Absalom Jones is the first Black priest ordained in the Episcopal Church.

1863
The Emancipation Proclamation is issued by President Abraham Lincoln, freeing enslaved people in the Southern states.

1865
The Thirteenth Amendment is passed, abolishing slavery in the United States.

(Continued)

Timeline of African Americans and the Episcopal Church (Continued)

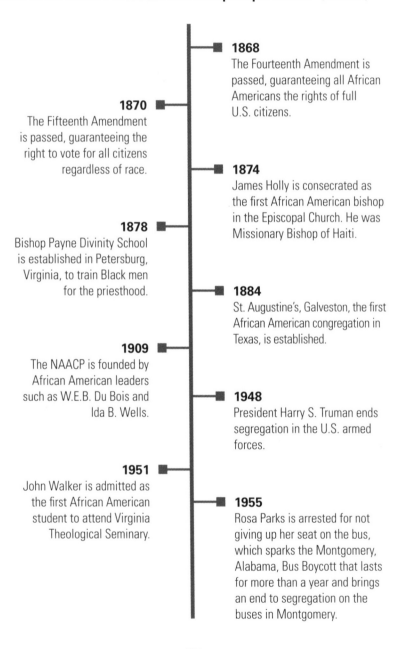

1868
The Fourteenth Amendment is passed, guaranteeing all African Americans the rights of full U.S. citizens.

1870
The Fifteenth Amendment is passed, guaranteeing the right to vote for all citizens regardless of race.

1874
James Holly is consecrated as the first African American bishop in the Episcopal Church. He was Missionary Bishop of Haiti.

1878
Bishop Payne Divinity School is established in Petersburg, Virginia, to train Black men for the priesthood.

1884
St. Augustine's, Galveston, the first African American congregation in Texas, is established.

1909
The NAACP is founded by African American leaders such as W.E.B. Du Bois and Ida B. Wells.

1948
President Harry S. Truman ends segregation in the U.S. armed forces.

1951
John Walker is admitted as the first African American student to attend Virginia Theological Seminary.

1955
Rosa Parks is arrested for not giving up her seat on the bus, which sparks the Montgomery, Alabama, Bus Boycott that lasts for more than a year and brings an end to segregation on the buses in Montgomery.

Timeline of African Americans and the Episcopal Church (Continued)

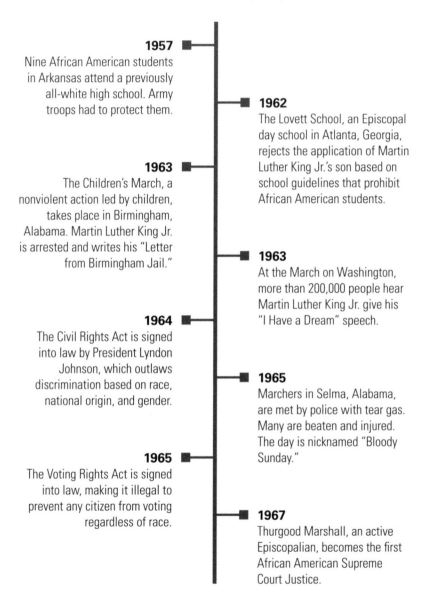

1957
Nine African American students in Arkansas attend a previously all-white high school. Army troops had to protect them.

1962
The Lovett School, an Episcopal day school in Atlanta, Georgia, rejects the application of Martin Luther King Jr.'s son based on school guidelines that prohibit African American students.

1963
The Children's March, a nonviolent action led by children, takes place in Birmingham, Alabama. Martin Luther King Jr. is arrested and writes his "Letter from Birmingham Jail."

1963
At the March on Washington, more than 200,000 people hear Martin Luther King Jr. give his "I Have a Dream" speech.

1964
The Civil Rights Act is signed into law by President Lyndon Johnson, which outlaws discrimination based on race, national origin, and gender.

1965
Marchers in Selma, Alabama, are met by police with tear gas. Many are beaten and injured. The day is nicknamed "Bloody Sunday."

1965
The Voting Rights Act is signed into law, making it illegal to prevent any citizen from voting regardless of race.

1967
Thurgood Marshall, an active Episcopalian, becomes the first African American Supreme Court Justice.

(Continued)

Timeline of African Americans and the Episcopal Church (Continued)

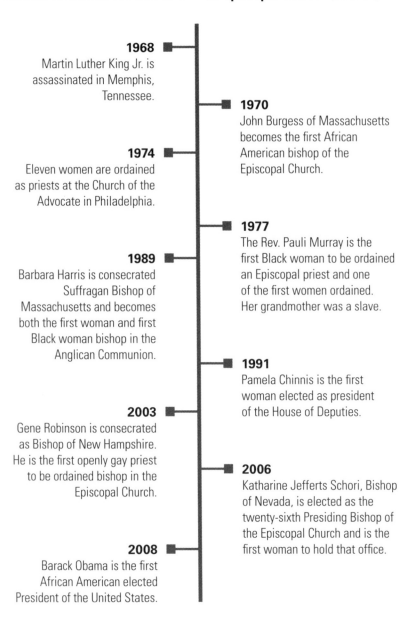

1968
Martin Luther King Jr. is assassinated in Memphis, Tennessee.

1970
John Burgess of Massachusetts becomes the first African American bishop of the Episcopal Church.

1974
Eleven women are ordained as priests at the Church of the Advocate in Philadelphia.

1977
The Rev. Pauli Murray is the first Black woman to be ordained an Episcopal priest and one of the first women ordained. Her grandmother was a slave.

1989
Barbara Harris is consecrated Suffragan Bishop of Massachusetts and becomes both the first woman and first Black woman bishop in the Anglican Communion.

1991
Pamela Chinnis is the first woman elected as president of the House of Deputies.

2003
Gene Robinson is consecrated as Bishop of New Hampshire. He is the first openly gay priest to be ordained bishop in the Episcopal Church.

2006
Katharine Jefferts Schori, Bishop of Nevada, is elected as the twenty-sixth Presiding Bishop of the Episcopal Church and is the first woman to hold that office.

2008
Barack Obama is the first African American elected President of the United States.

Timeline of African Americans and the Episcopal Church (Continued)

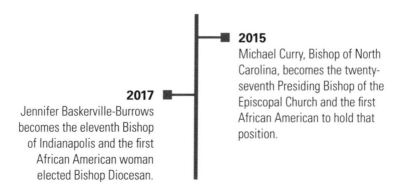

2015
Michael Curry, Bishop of North Carolina, becomes the twenty-seventh Presiding Bishop of the Episcopal Church and the first African American to hold that position.

2017
Jennifer Baskerville-Burrows becomes the eleventh Bishop of Indianapolis and the first African American woman elected Bishop Diocesan.

A Few Words about My Art

I want to publicly thank Rev. Bozzuti-Jones for the opportunity to participate in the creation of this wonderful project. Father Mark, through his continued patronage, witnessed the transformation of a comic book artist and character designer into a digital portrait painter. It's been an interesting and sometimes arduous journey, but one I'm glad I've taken. I'd like to think that *Absalom Jones: America's First Black Priest* is the culmination of both disciplines. Whereas the cover speaks to a modernized and unique interpretation, the interior work harkens back to my comic illustrator roots—which is fitting given that this book is first and foremost for children.

Christopher Michael Taylor